SlowRoad

Poems *by* Sheila Templeton

ISBN 0 9547084 3 1

Acknowledgement is made to the editors of the following publications, where some of these poems first appeared:
New Writing Scotland, The Herald, Poetry Scotland.

Design by Brian Craig
b.c@briancraig.demon.co.uk

Printed at Anderson & Sons Stationers Ltd
34 Loanbank Quadrant, Govan, Glasgow G51 3HZ.

Published by Makar Press, Troon, Ayrshire.

Contents

For my grandfather
Alec Edward
and my son
Aleks Jurczyk,
with much love
and thanks.

Thanks also to my family, friends and fellow writers, especially the other members of Makar Press, for their support, encouragement and editorial advice. To my friends Brian and Alison Craig, not only for the typography and design of this collection, but also much holding of the fort and all round supervision, my most grateful thanks and appreciation.

Haiku for **St Bridget's Day**

Wind hustles the last
of winter from the street.
Tissue birds fly.

Snow drops bunch up
along the bank, making space
for Spring.

Haiku for **Spring**

Spring sun strokes green
into new willow.
Catkins purr.

A slither of sun
opens my dull window.
Waves zigzag, sparkling.

Going **Home**

Peesie weeps and whaups shrieking,
wheeling high above ploughed parks.
Granda's calloused hand holds mine.
We are watching oyster catchers
mincing in the shining shallow
waters of the quartz pebbled Don.

He wears faded flapping dungarees
with a craftsman's special pocket.
His bonnet covers bumpy bits
and narrow strands of hair. I lean
against his smell, freshly dusted
sawdust, mixed through
Capstan Navy Full Strength.

We wonder at a salmon glistening
on a bed of fragrant weed.
Then like a serving spoon
the river flips it over.
We see what's underneath.

'Ach. Otters are right bonny beasts
but they're selfish wee buggers.'

He shows me distant Bennachie
with Mither Tap glassing
black against its clouds. I listen
rapt to tales of vanished tribes
who built tall fires there, who
knew how to melt rock
and weld stones forever.

Then going home planting
my feet in Granda's prints,
in that careful space
down the side of a park
filled with young green corn.

Summertime

Summertime was the unmarried aunts
hurrying in from the ice cream van,
their booty of vanilla piled high
in an old baking bowl,
like a wedding celebration
melting in laughter.

Straightening stocking seams,
they shouted for lemonade, better still
a big bottle of American Cream Soda,
long spoons and the tallest glasses
from the kitchen press.

We sat outside, legs dangling
from a scarred bench made of old
railway sleepers, stirring our floats

pearling clear glass with sticky strands
set forever in beaded DNA of memory.

Beeswax

My nose is greedy
grasping for the fix
of buttery rich beeswax.
Yellow cream order
brings the comfort of
scratched key-patterned
lino, mixed up with
sharp smells from
the press in the lobby,
where I first breathed in
the dark rich blood
of the hare draining
into a bowl.
The thick brown soup
of my childhood;
taken for granted
along with firm white
whole King Edwards.
Cutting mashing them
through velvet strands.
I, the guileless gourmet
supped it all up.

Daddy's **Girl** _____

You were Alan Ladd. All chiselled
cheekbones and blond hair falling
into your eyes. I had no idea
you towered above him.
You towered over everybody.

At tea time I raced to meet you
my legs carefully bowed.
'Born in the saddle' you'd drawl
each day, sounding amazed.

We'd saddle up and gallop
through our canyon, chasing
maverick steers around the kitchen
until the ding of a chow wagon triangle
brought us sweaty to the table,
pushing stetsons back, hitching
horses to the old oak dresser.

'Pork an' beans AGAIN'
you'd say, looking down
at brimming plates of broth.
'No, pardner. Tonight,
it's beans and pork!'
Slapping our knees in glee
knowing who we were.

Until the night of my first
school Christmas party,
where in my new blue silk
dress and butterfly hair slides
suddenly you couldn't see me.

But I always knew you.
You were Alan Ladd.

Mother's **Lipstick**

It never looked new, always worn
to a lip smoothed point, sharper
on one side. Movie star red.
The case was shiny gilt,
set with chips of diamond glass
like the stars in a cinema ceiling.

My ten-year-old eyes reflected
their glint, as you swivelled up
a quarter inch of carmine.
All you allowed. Just enough
to cover your wide mouth.

Then that little finger furtively
skilfully rubbing away all trace
of bold girl pout, so your mouth
was somehow poppy innocent.
That was as far as you could go.

In my glossy youth I took charge,
painting on lavish colour, outlining
how it should be done.
You smiled and thanked me.
But the giveaway was always
the flush on the tip of your pinkie.

I gave up trying to make you over.
And you've been gone for years.

So it was a shock yesterday
to find my own little finger busy
at the mirror, rubbing, smudging.
As if all along, it knew my mouth
better than I do.

Wolfman _____

You had to wear it straight away,
going home. A whole month's
pocket money.
Innocent drivers paled at Wolfman
sitting by my side and we laughed.

That was the Hallowe'en we cried
and shouted at each other, when
we discovered even my fixing fingers
couldn't stick enough hairs
to wolf mat your smooth paws.
And made up over a pair
of customised old gloves.

Then I waited,
for your glory flushed face above
a bag of sticky night treasure
untasted as you began planning
next year's triumph.

'Start growin' ma hair NOW
to gell up for Dracula. An' buy
fangs an' greeny-white face
stuff an' can you sew a cloak
a real one... swishy... with
a red silk lining?'

Children are chapping on
my darkened door.
I should be putting out
bowls for nuts and apples,
arranging little towers of silver.

But I sit here seeing you prowling,
padding around faraway streets,
swishing that new student cloak.
And I wonder how can it be
Hallowe'en, while Wolfman
lies in his box upstairs.

Like a **Visitor**

Your room's tidy.
You've left it
downie smoothed,
pillow sitting up
like a plump visitor.

I'm glad of this damp towel
crumpling a corner.

'Okay to have a bath', you said.

Okay was you
sprawling careless limbs,
sloth draped
over the settee.
A cornflake mountain
drowned in milk.
Locust stripped fridge,
Dead Head Comics,
flicking T.V. channels,
driving me daft.
Not hearing
until I squatted down
into your eyeballs.

'What's that you're sayin', Mum?'

I'm saying,

That time you slammed
a fist into thin wall,
and you... wet newspaper,
chalky plaster mixed
in a jam jar,
tongue sticking out
in concentration,
covering the hole,

'Calm down Mother. It's fine!'

Has left a space,
an empty place.
My hand finds it,
every time I climb
these stairs.

A bumpy, gritty patch,
unpainted and never
sanded smooth.

When Will You Come?

(After reading of the African woman
 to be stoned to death for bearing
a child out of wedlock.)

You will have to come for me
in darkness. How could you stand
the light? And who among you
will cast the first stone?

Will it be you, Abdullah, closing
your bread shop and your mind
long enough to hurry to that place.
Long enough to forget your kindness
of honey pastries and sweet yellow
date cakes, slipped quietly in my basket.

Or you, Nurgis, who eased my child
into this world, helped her fill
her lungs for her first breath.
Will you be running, holding
a heavy stone in both hands?

Like the one used each day
by our courtyard song thrush,
the one surrounded by broken
stained snail shells.

You say this can wait until my daughter
is weaned. I thank you for that.

But who will feed her in the morning?

Window Seat

The train rackets me forwards
creaking, hissing, as it paints
black and white cows standing
against a rain green field.

Wipes them out.

A swan flashes a dazzling sail
bottom up in a dull stretch of water.
Mist keeps the far valley secret.

Evaporates.

Speed carves a rearing horse
nostrils wide, mane braided
with tiny pearl drops.

Out of a dead tree.

Orderly windows march by,
three deep, reflecting the buffed
gleam of a clean washed sky.

In the distance.

Graffiti blocked in scarlet and white,
a clown's square mouth, glares
and shouts 'Tongs Ya Bass'.

Can't touch me.

Stationary **Haiku** _____

Central Station
where this train shall terminate.
ZAP! K-POW!

Beach **Haiku** _____

Dark seaweed tossed up
in a frondy moustache
smiles at me.

I Looked for Winter

I looked for winter in this place,
walking, walking by an icy sea,
my black coat flying.

Found endings in bear pelts
of drowned grass, in beached
bladderwrack gasping at my feet.

Bowed my head beside slabs
of elephant skin rock, long folded,
crouching in silent witness.

But the sea, having none of it,
throws a bathful of stinging salt,
laughs at me dripping.

Garlands sand in wild ribbons
of toffee slick kelp. Plops down
jellyfish fed by amber sun,

lighting the way to the party.

Hot **Chick** _____

Ma man sez
'Yer... HOT.'
Ah sez 'Mmm'
in his ear.
He sez 'Naw,
yer HOT, ah mean
sizzlin', hen, ah
could fry an egg
oan yer back.
Whit's wrang,
ur ye no weel?
It's no verra comfy
fur me.
Yer like a toasty
hot water bottle
a' the time.
Iz this whit thon
Germaine Greer
cries The Change?
Ur you huvven
a hot flush?'

'Naw', ah sez,
'ah'm huvven
a Power Surge.
An' you kin sleep
on the flerr.'

A Little **Sleeve**

These are not my arms,
these lardy bits, bulging.

They grew in the night.
Along with trailing wings
like a lizard's webbed oxter.

Maybe if I paint
my nails
HOT
SCARLET?

Sit all evening,
elbows bent,
firming the droops.

'Madam, a little sleeve is
so nice... on the older lady.'

Fuck your little sleeve.
There's my frock.
There.
That one.
The rhinestone satin...
with the shoe string straps.

Language **of Loss** _____

There is no protection from memory's loose cannon.
My kitchen was anything but safe today. I stood
innocently tearing off silver wrap for left overs
and with no invitation you appeared, spreading

a clean sheet of foil over your well used grill pan.
No time to scrape any more leavings of the old year.
It was half an hour to midnight and everything
still to be done. Cocktail sausages gleaming pink,

the ritual of nippy white onions to be speared
in between cubes of yellow sweating cheese
and dripping sweet chunks of pineapple.
You laughing at the impossibility of it all.

The language of loss has no words. It is a hand
raised unaware to the bony place below the throat
where skin stretches thin over my breast bone.
It is my whole body bent in two, trying to keep

the two halves of my heart together, as though
grief can possibly be contained.

Indigo **Nightmare**_____

It needed the thick dark
that presses on your face
so soft your tongue wants
to lick there. Eyes stroked asleep
by trusting darkness, limbs
uncurling like a sea anemone
in deep water, drifting unaware
into what was waiting.

There were steps, worn stone
with no rail, so my left hand
trailed up the solid wall
of home as I climbed.
It was cold there, a smirr
of sleet needling my face.
The top step promised safety.
A door facing me, the sound
of a kettle singing.

My hand reached up,
strained for the door knob.
A sharp edge of old brass
caught, scratched damp fingers.
I held it tight, started to turn.

Then the last step liquefied
under my feet, the sickening
lurch over the edge.
That moment of falling
falling forever, through
infinite space, knowing
with certainty I was dead.

Yet opening eyes
against purple blue sleep,
tangled still in the white
of the sheets and the dreaming,
alone on a cold hard floor.

Samhain

It is the time, Mither.
I can bide nae longer. Too late
now tae break your solemn word.
You gied him it and so did I.

At Samhain feast each year,
I leave this world and go wi' him.
The bower o'simmer time maun wither,
starry gowans blackenin the grass,
while you wander half deid wi' grief,
lettin not a blade live till I return.
Apples are piled sweet, the hairst
gaithered dry, the cattle safely
in for the lang lang nichts tae come.
You ken fine I have to go.

The flames of the Shannock fire
are leapin, bleezin in ma hert.
My work is feenished here.

I sat wi' the maidens, nicht efter
nicht, making fine thin bannocks.
Passed them hand tae hand,
toasting each one for the feast.
I watched them toss the hazel nuts
on tae hot girdles, scarce breathin
lookin tae find their ain true love.
Will they dance together? Or apart?
It's all one tae me. Tears or joy.
I maun leave. He is waiting.

This is sair, Mither.
I love the simmer time.
I miss your airms aboot me,
twined like a summer vine.

But I'd be tellin a lee if I denied
when that big black coach
o' his comes steerin blawin
up through the grun and
him standing at the reins, stern
and dark, sooty ravens cawin
their welcome, that ma hert
hemmers like a wild caged
bird against my ribs, thinking
how it will be wi' him.

Bringing Grunnie Up To Date

There must have been a telegram.
Did you open it, ashen faced
or did you ask your mither?
You stood in that warm kitchen
a hand up at your throat,
and you opened it.

No comfort in War Office
speak. You knew a shell
had practically blaa'n him
tae smithereens in Flanders mud
richt in front, wi' the ither sappers
buildin' duckboards, parapets.
Shoring up the impossible.

You couldna thole the waiting.
You packed. Dressed the bairns.
[Silent mither watching.]
Caught the train fae Aiberdeen.
You'd never been in Glasgow.
The cabby was kind. 'Gie me that.
I'll see you tae the Ayr train.'

Through misted swaying glass
you saw that parks in Ayrshire
sweep green doon to the sea
like at Balmedie. And burnies
rin clear, bubbling ower polished
stanes. The rhythm o' the train
thudding like your heart.

Where will we bide?
Will Ayr be close enough
tae Ballochmyle Hospital?
What if... I canna love
whatever he is now.

Every day for six months, you
attended him, keeping them quiet.
Even bocht silk thread and needles
for sewing simple samplers
to keep some kind of peace.

The day came the doctor
said he could try a walk.
Slowly you two hirpled
around the grounds. Now you
kent for sure he wid be hale.
You prayed. Fierce faced, knees
sair on cauld linoleum.

Please God
Let him nae be sent back. I will niver
complain again. No, not ever.
For the rest of my life. Amen.

The day when you managed the sea side.
And there you are in crackled sepia
the little girls laughing, button boots off
standing ankle deep in water. Winnie
looking out under her wild frizz. Peggy,
velvet ribbon sliding off straight corn silk.
(My own mother not yet made.)

Now I live beside that beach,
wade in the same sea.
I look at your captured faces
and wonder what brought
me to this place.

It's a mystery. Like those knots
of purple tissue, cocooned shrapnel
behind his ear and curling there,
on the back of his left hand.